THIS BOOK BELONGS TO

_____

FOR THE KIDS WHO WANT TO WIN

ISBN: 9798894582191

YOUNG THOMAS RODE WITH HIS FELLOW KNIGHTS, THE TEMPLARS, ACROSS THE HOT DESERT. THEY CARRIED HEAVY ARMOR, THEIR BANNERS FLYING HIGH.

THE SUN BURNED BRIGHT ABOVE THEM. THOMAS DREAMED OF HOME—GREEN HILLS, COOL RIVERS, AND HIS FAMILY WAITING FOR HIS RETURN.

SUDDENLY, SHOUTS FILLED THE AIR. ARROWS FLEW PAST.
THE ENEMY WAS NEAR! THE TEMPLARS PREPARED FOR BATTLE.

THE FIGHT WAS FIERCE. THOMAS SWUNG HIS SWORD,
HIS HEART POUNDING. BUT SOON, HE WAS SURROUNDED.

A SARACEN WARRIOR POINTED A CURVED SWORD AT THOMAS. "SURRENDER, " THE WARRIOR SAID. THOMAS DROPPED HIS WEAPON.

HE WAS LED AWAY, HANDS TIED. HIS HEART SANK.
WHAT WOULD HAPPEN TO HIM NOW?

IN A GRAND CITY, THOMAS WAS TAKEN TO A SCHOLAR NAMED IDRIS.
"YOU ARE SAFE," IDRIS SAID GENTLY. "DO NOT FEAR."

THOMAS DID NOT TRUST IDRIS. "YOU ARE MY ENEMY," HE SAID.
IDRIS ONLY SMILED AND POURED HIM COOL WATER.

DAYS PASSED. IDRIS SHOWED THOMAS BOOKS WITH STRANGE SYMBOLS.
"THESE ARE WORDS," IDRIS EXPLAINED. "THEY HOLD GREAT KNOWLEDGE."

THOMAS WATCHED AS IDRIS WROTE WITH INK AND A REED PEN.
HE HAD NEVER SEEN SUCH WRITING BEFORE.

"CAN YOU READ?" IDRIS ASKED. THOMAS SHOOK HIS HEAD.
"THEN I WILL TEACH YOU," IDRIS SAID.

AT FIRST, THE LETTERS MADE NO SENSE. BUT SLOWLY, THOMAS BEGAN TO UNDERSTAND. HE COULD READ SIMPLE WORDS.

IDRIS ALSO TAUGHT THOMAS ABOUT STARS. "THEY GUIDE TRAVELERS AT NIGHT," IDRIS SAID, POINTING TO THE SKY.

THOMAS LISTENED CAREFULLY. HE HAD ALWAYS THOUGHT KNIGHTS WERE THE WISEST, BUT IDRIS KNEW SO MUCH MORE.

ONE EVENING, IDRIS BROUGHT THOMAS A PLATE OF FOOD. "TASTE THIS, " HE SAID. THE SPICES WERE STRANGE BUT DELICIOUS.

"THERE IS MUCH TO LEARN BEYOND BATTLE," IDRIS SAID. "BOOKS, STARS, FOOD—ALL ARE PART OF THE WORLD."

THOMAS THOUGHT OF HIS OWN TEACHERS BACK HOME.
THEY NEVER SPOKE OF THESE THINGS.

ONE DAY, IDRIS ASKED, "WHAT DO YOU MISS MOST?"
THOMAS HESITATED. "MY HOME," HE SAID AT LAST.

"A HOME IS MORE THAN LAND," IDRIS SAID.
"IT IS WHAT WE CARRY IN OUR HEARTS."

THOMAS FELT CONFUSED. HE HAD ALWAYS BELIEVED HOME WAS WHERE HIS PEOPLE LIVED, BUT NOW HE WASN'T SURE.

MORE TIME PASSED. THOMAS NO LONGER FELT LIKE A PRISONER.
HE AND IDRIS SHARED STORIES AND LAUGHED TOGETHER.

ONE DAY, IDRIS TOOK THOMAS OUTSIDE THE CITY. "WATCH,
" IDRIS SAID, POINTING TO A CARAVAN OF TRADERS.

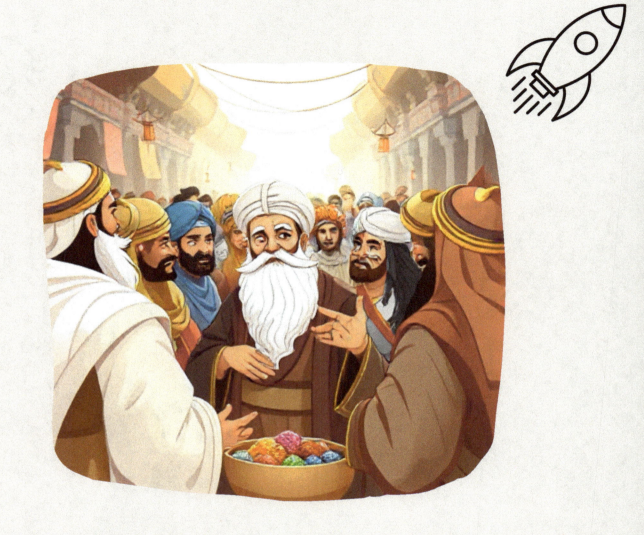

MEN FROM DIFFERENT LANDS SPOKE MANY LANGUAGES. "THEY TRADE, SHARE, AND LEARN FROM EACH OTHER," IDRIS EXPLAINED.

THOMAS HAD ALWAYS BEEN TOLD THE SARACENS WERE ENEMIES.
BUT THESE PEOPLE DID NOT SEEM LIKE ENEMIES AT ALL.

ONE EVENING, IDRIS SAID, "IT IS TIME FOR YOU TO CHOOSE—STAY HERE OR RETURN TO YOUR PEOPLE."

THOMAS'S HEART ACHED. HE WANTED TO SEE HIS FAMILY,
BUT HE ALSO WANTED TO LEARN MORE.

"YOU ARE NOT THE SAME BOY WHO ARRIVED HERE," IDRIS SAID.
"YOU SEE THE WORLD WITH NEW EYES."

THOMAS THOUGHT OF THE BOOKS, THE STARS, THE STORIES,
AND THE KINDNESS HE HAD FOUND HERE.

"I WANT TO RETURN HOME," THOMAS SAID, "BUT I WILL NEVER FORGET WHAT I HAVE LEARNED."

IDRIS NODDED. "THEN GO WITH AN OPEN HEART. BE A BRIDGE, NOT A WALL."

THE NEXT MORNING, THOMAS SET OUT. HE CARRIED NO
SWORD, ONLY A SMALL BOOK FROM IDRIS.

HIS JOURNEY HOME WAS LONG. AS HE TRAVELED, HE WATCHED THE STARS AND READ THE BOOK BY FIRELIGHT.

AT LAST, THOMAS REACHED HIS HOMELAND.
HIS FAMILY REJOICED, BUT HE FELT DIFFERENT.

HE SHARED STORIES OF WHAT HE HAD LEARNED—ABOUT STARS, BOOKS, AND THE KINDNESS OF STRANGERS.

AT FIRST, PEOPLE DID NOT BELIEVE HIM. "THE
SARACENS ARE OUR ENEMIES," THEY SAID.

"NOT ALL OF THEM," THOMAS REPLIED. "THERE IS WISDOM
BEYOND OUR WALLS. WE MUST LISTEN AND LEARN."

SOME LAUGHED, BUT OTHERS LISTENED. SLOWLY,
THOMAS'S WORDS BEGAN TO SPREAD.

HE TAUGHT CHILDREN TO READ, JUST AS IDRIS HAD TAUGHT HIM. HE TOLD KNIGHTS OF THE STARS.

YEARS PASSED. THOMAS BECAME A GREAT TEACHER.
HE NEVER FORGOT HIS TIME WITH IDRIS.

AND ON CLEAR NIGHTS, HE LOOKED UP AT THE STARS, REMEMBERING THE FRIEND WHO HAD ONCE SHOWN HIM THE WAY.